TAD CARPENTER

Sunday Suns

Counter-Print Books

Hello Sunshine

This project is an experiment. This project is play. This project is half therapy and half visual journalism. This project is a small way to inject our world with some much needed positivity and light.

Truth be told, I have always felt the most at peace with myself when making something. I love the feeling of getting totally lost in the act of creating something that didn't exist the day before. Getting the opportunity to make something for someone and do so everyday for a living is a gift. Maybe it's not a new iPhone, but a gift nonetheless. Several years ago, I found myself slowly beginning to doubt my own creative abilities, and honestly, doubt my own self-worth because of it. Why was this happening? Why was I evaluating my personal worth against my creative output? I couldn't understand how I went from being a seemingly confident, self-employed designer of 10+ years to someone who began questioning literally every mark and every move I made. Was it the 24/7 scrolling culture I was part of? Was it career overload and burnout? Was it the current toxic America I was in no way immune to?

As a partner of a brand design studio that I co-run with my wife, I can truly say I love very much what we get to do for a living. Our studio really does take on the type of work I have always wanted. We design the type of work I can 100% stand behind and enjoy making. But, over time, the daily rejection and scrutiny I encountered in a world dictated by economic success can take a toll on a sensitive little artist like myself. In 2015, I found myself struggling and frequently getting down on myself. As a human, I was feeling overwhelmed, anxious, depressed, off, all of the emotional catchphrases you can think of, insert them here. All was going great, yet I was not feeling like myself and I didn't know why exactly. I began to feel guilty for feeling this way. I personally knew that I needed to confront my insecurities and feelings head on (in addition to confiding in people I trusted). These feelings affected my work as if a wave of anxiety and doubt was rolling into my creative process like a hurricane. I was throwing myself a pity party that had become an epic rager. The cops needed to be called to break it up. It was time to down that last beer, run out the back door and head home before curfew. But how do I get home?

After a very long stressful week, one Sunday morning I found myself unable to sleep. Tossing and turning for hours, I finally pulled myself out of bed and ventured to my home studio in the darkness of early morning. I thought I could get a head start on the week and begin revising some work for a client. Instead, I found myself not moving at all but just gazing out the window like some kind of generic sad boy in a stock photo. I sat there still, doing nothing, in the dark and watched the sun rise. While feeling overwhelmed, beaten down and maybe even a little lost, it dawned on me (yes, dawned that was a bad sun pun—get used to them), we as people tend to find joy when we are doing something we love. It's often that simple. It's even something we are taught as children, "just go play" adults would tell us. I personally always thought my mom was just trying to get me to leave her alone when she asked me to go play outside. But maybe, just maybe, we were learning something much more important in those neighborhood wiffleball games. When we play we are honestly at our most happy. We are being taught from the very youngest of age to seek moments to play. "Go color" Mom would say. "Go play outside" Dad would shout. "Go build a fort, ride a bike, read a book, find a dead body" (wait, that last one was the plot of *Stand By Me*, scratch that one). Play has long been believed to reinforce imagination, creativity, dexterity and emotional strength. But could it really be that easy? Just start playing more and POOF, we'll be better? I am not naive enough to think it is that easy, but it is a good place to start. Maybe I really do need to inject more play into my life and work? Maybe we all do?

I decided to designate a specific time every week for me to just play. If I didn't create these rules it would be hard for me to follow through. Setting up boundaries helps us all be more accountable towards our goals. I also needed a subject, a thing I could use as a vehicle to play within and through—something that could be used like a vessel to pour meaning into. I wanted something that skewed positive yet was broad and adaptive. That Sunday morning, after sitting in the dark staring away like a sad, 90's emo kid, I started designing a single sun for me and no one else. I had no plan, no creative brief, no client, no rules, no restrictions—just me, design and play. Every week I injected this act into my life, it made me feel a little bit better about myself and my craft. By forcing my brain to look at the world through a more positive, sunny lens it helped me see the light (see, more sun-puns). Sometimes it really can be as simple as thinking positive leads to being positive.

> **"I had no plan, no creative brief, no client, no rules, no restrictions—just me, design and play. Every week I injected this act into my life, it made me feel a little bit better about myself and my craft."**

This project has given me some powerful rewards by carving out time to create a simple sun for a couple of hours each week. It has given me permission to reflect on my feelings. It has become a vehicle to express myself and the environment around me. It has become a great way to experiment with styles which has led to new and different types of work. It has thoroughly given me a sense of clarity. However, maybe the most important and unexpected aspect of this self-reflective experiment is how these little suns have provided hope to others.

Tad Carpenter
Carpenter Collective

"By forcing my brain to look at the world through a more positive, sunny lens it helped me see the light. Sometimes it really can be as simple as thinking positive leads to being positive."

Spring

We had no idea how to organize this book, I want to be very honest about that. We explored so many different ideas and highly technical design solutions. We started with the idea to collate all the suns by style, or maybe by material, or maybe we keep them in sequential order? Actually, maybe we just throw all the suns up in the air and see where they land? In the end, we allowed the sun itself to help us organize the work. As we all know, this spinning marble we call home revolves around the sun and as its sunlight hits different parts of our planet, it creates seasons. These four seasons seemed like a logical way to share and organize this six year long experiment.

When you think about it, Spring really is the most arrogant and narcissistic of the four seasons. After all, this is the season that turns cold stuff to warm stuff. This is the season that actually creates life and magically triggers buds to grow on trees and bushes everywhere. Birds literally start racing into our orbit to sing and enjoy this magical, what seems like a two week long, season. Spring, even in all it's vanity, is a symbol of hope and resurrection. Don't worry people, I'm not going to get preachy. I would be the last person you should look to for guidance in bettering yourself. However, Spring's message of hope and its highly narcissistic behavior does strike a chord with me. I did in fact start this project to better MYSELF as a designer, to make MYSELF feel better, to share what I HAD TO SAY. Wow, who's the narcissist now, Spring?

No matter who you are or how you are feeling, this flower and pastel covered season fills your heart with hope and happiness. Spring sweeps away doubt and coldness and fills our bones with warmth. It also fills our lungs with seasonal allergies and our days with Spring cleaning, thanks for nothing, Febreeze. My hope is that the suns I created over the past six Springs also bring you warmth, hope and only the subtlest aroma of cheap odor eliminator.

These buttons were made for inchxinch.org with proceeds going to multiple charities that impact young artists and encourage the value of the arts.

**Me to my computer:
"OK, let's make some good
graphic design today!"**

**Narrator:
"He did not make good
graphic design today."**

I skipped the gym this morning but the good news is I've probably scrolled at least 2-3 miles already today on my phone.

In honor of NCAA
March Madness.

In honor of Mother's Day.
Especially, in honor of my
mom, Rebecca Carpenter.
I love you, Mom.

Momma knows Best

OPTIMISTIC

Negative thoughts will never give you a positive outcome.

In honor of our one year anniversary. One full orbit around the sun.

Summer

Heck yeah, it's summer! Oh wait, I'm an adult and have a job, never mind...

What I really love about the suns I created during the Summers is that this group, more than any other, feels like a personal journal or diary. Not the juicy older sister crush diary, but a documentation of all the travel and special events that took place during these bright, warmer days.

One of the challenges I liked about this project was figuring out how I was going to create a sun while on the road. It could be as simple as bringing a sketchbook with me, or something more complex like planning ahead and creating a custom plush toy design to bring along. My mom and I collaborated on a custom, wool plush sun that I brought with me to Singapore where I spoke at a conference.

I thought it would be fun to bring it along and take photos of it all over beautiful Singapore as we visited. Quickly, I found out that people saw me doing this and they wanted to know what I was doing, or why I was doing it. It became a simple way to break the ice and have conversations with people from the other side of the globe. Without the help of this little plush sun, I may not have been able to meet and connect with people along our trip.

Just in the summers alone, I made suns in Singapore, Thailand, Italy, Germany, New Orleans, Minneapolis, Las Vegas, Austin and Dallas Texas. Summers are also for celebrating—Father's Day, the upcoming birth of my son, 4th of July and lots of celebrations of love. So even if you used up all your vacation days on hangovers and TV binging, let this little trip be on me.

Reach out to someone you've
lost touch with, just to say Hi.

SUMMER

SHINETOWN

Pool & Tub **CLEANING**

1-800-555-2424

IT'S ALWAYS SHINE TIME ● CALL FOR A FREE QUOTE
NOW ACCEPTING CREDIT CARDS!

A hand painted sun mural
for our son.

Graphic Design is 70% being creative and 42% being glad there's very minimal math.

Made in collaboration with
my beautiful, talented mother,
fiber-artist Becki Carpenter.
All wool hand dyed and
rug hooked.

Hello from Singapore! Hand-
made sun plush toy I made
in collaboration with my
mom, Rebecca Carpenter.

Because we could all use a little
peace and love right now.

A two color screen print given to all attending my talk at Creative Mornings KC.

SUMMER

THINKING POSITIVE IS BEING **POSITIVE**

PRINTED BY VAHALLA STUDIOS IN KANSAS CITY

Tad Carpenter

Office morale has increased substantially since we started holding New Orleans style jazz funerals for all our rejected designs.

TAD CARPENTER

TC

Made while en route
to Frankfurt, Germany.
Auf Wiedersehen!

40 Days of Dating   Timothy Goodman & Jessica Walsh

ABRAMS

THINGS I HAVE LEARNE
STEFAN SAGMEISTER

TIMOTHY GOODMAN
CHRONICLE BOOKS

SHARPIE ART WORKSHOP   CREATIVE PEP TALK

Staying up past midnight is the new hangover.

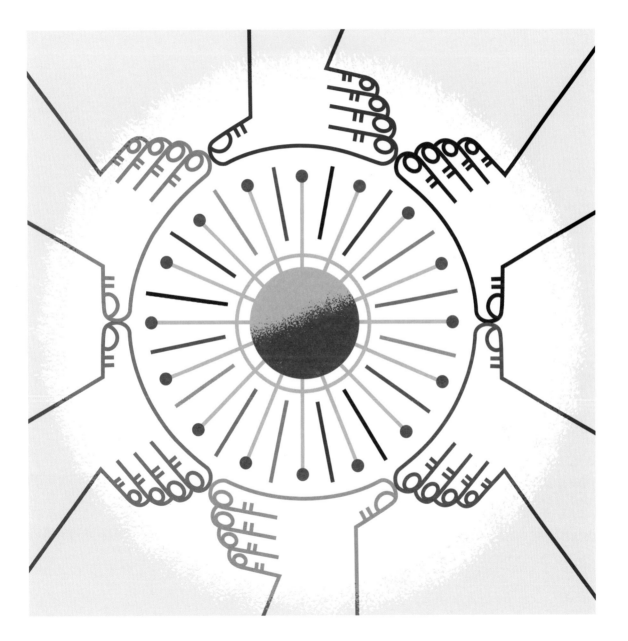

Fall

We get it, Fall is your favorite season. I mean, I get it, just look around. The colors are beautiful, there's a crispness in the air, you get to pull out that cool chunky *When Harry Met Sally* sweater out of retirement and the leaves. Oh those leaves. Leaves might be our favorite dead thing to ooh and aah over, right after the Grateful Dead of course. If Fall was in the Olympics, it would surely be standing at the tallest part of the winners' podium with a gold medal draped around its leafy neck. Sorry Winter, you finish fourth.

Many of the designs I made in the Fall use these warm Autumn colors, because I am so darn original. It was partially not my fault, as you will see a lot of these suns were made while celebrating or partaking in Fall activities. For example, several suns were made during or after big hiking trips. I do enjoy hiking but whoever invented it, I want to hire them immediately—they're

a genius. Not because this is such a creative activity to invent but the exact opposite, this Billy Mays salesman basically just talked us all into getting excited to go walking. Walking. That thing we do all the time and frankly, try to avoid (I love you airport moving walkways). When I hiked at Zion National Park and kissed the ground once I completed Angel's Landing (Google it, why did I do this?), I brought a small sketchbook to sit and doodle my weekly sun. Subsequently, when hiking the Grand Canyon I have to admit, I designed this several days after we hiked and not actually on a Sunday. I feel awful about this, but it does feel good to get off my chest.

Expect pumpkins, gourds, turkeys, candy corn and yes, leaves. Lots and lots of leaves. I guess adding leaves to a design is like when a musician just starts "wooing" in a song. It might not always be conceptually relevant but dang, it just feels good.

In honor of hiking
the Grand Canyon.

It's SONday! Because I became a father! Meet my SON, Luca James Carpenter.

Behind every super cool everything organized neatly photo is a messy pile of coffee cups, self doubt and fast food wrappers.*

***this is a metaphor for my creative process.**

DON'T BE A Cloud AND THROW SHADE

20s: Netflix and chill
30s: Netflix and antacids

NETFLIX

SEPTEMBER
FIFTH
1882

Routed out of plywood,
painted and hangs
at 3ft x 3ft.

FALL

Hand-painted mural in our
Carpenter Collective office.
Designed by my wife, Jessica
Carpenter and I.

SUNDAY SUNS

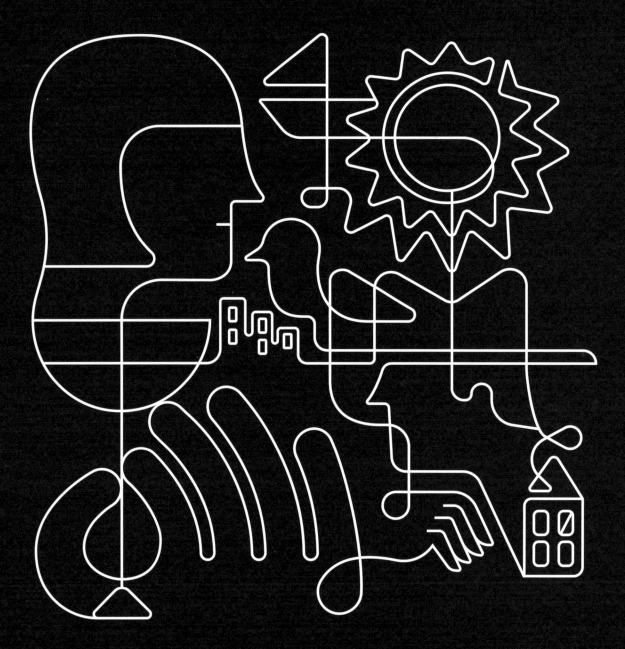

HUG SOMEONE SO TIGHT THAT ALL THEIR BROKEN PIECES JUST STICK BACK TOGETHER

LOOK for the GOOD

MORE Shine less → SHADE.

In response to a difficult week,
the 2016 US Presidential Election
and holding on to hope.

Hold on to that

Candy corn is by far my favorite vegetable.

Monday the 13th woulda been a much scarier film.

The only thing scaring me this Halloween is the number of unanswered emails in my inbox.

Winter

I think everyone's favorite winter activity is just complaining about winter. Yes, it's cold, yes it gets dark early and yes it makes you want to throw your arms up and say screw it, elastic pants forever. But I'm here to tell you, there are so many positives we forget to contribute to this snowy season. For example, we get to eat holiday cookies for breakfast, lunch and dinner without any judgment for like six straight weeks. The snow also makes it totally justified to skip almost any obligation (sorry, Facebook friend Brayden who I met once, I will not be attending your color-themed Blue Years Eve party). And lastly, family time. Nothing says winter like good ol' family dinners filled with love, awkwardness and enough new content to keep my therapist employed for the next year.

In all seriousness, I love the winter because of these family gatherings and traditions. You'll see many of the suns I made during the winter centered around these traditions, holidays and various winter events. Family means everything to me and everything I get to do is because of them. This chapter admittedly gets a little sappy—not like *Toy Story* 3 sappy but, maybe closer to John Hughes sappy. A kind of sappy that makes you smile and call your best friend from 6th grade to just see how the heck they've been doing.

Even as a commercial artist (which I believe is a bad word), I like to make work that says something. Even if that something is actually saying nothing. Several of the suns towards the end of this chapter honor my wife and how lucky I am to have her as my partner (I warned you, it's gonna get sappy). There is also a sun that I designed and was tattooed on a friend to honor her family. You can see her son and wife's initials hidden within the design. There are suns that honor Santa, political movements, new beginnings and our family's favorite Saturday tradition, making pancakes.

MISSING!

LAST SEEN: In the sky like maybe 5 months ago.

DESCRIPTION: Yellowish orange, is a nearly perfect sphere of hot plasma, is a dope source of energy for life on Earth. Generally pretty chill.

If seen please call a friend and go outside and do fun stuff.

Call a cool friend and go do cool stuff.
Call a cool friend and go do cool stuff.
Call a cool friend and go do cool stuff.
Call a cool friend and go do cool stuff.
Call a cool friend and go do cool stuff.
Call a cool friend and go do cool stuff.
Call a cool friend and go do cool stuff.
Call a cool friend and go do cool stuff.

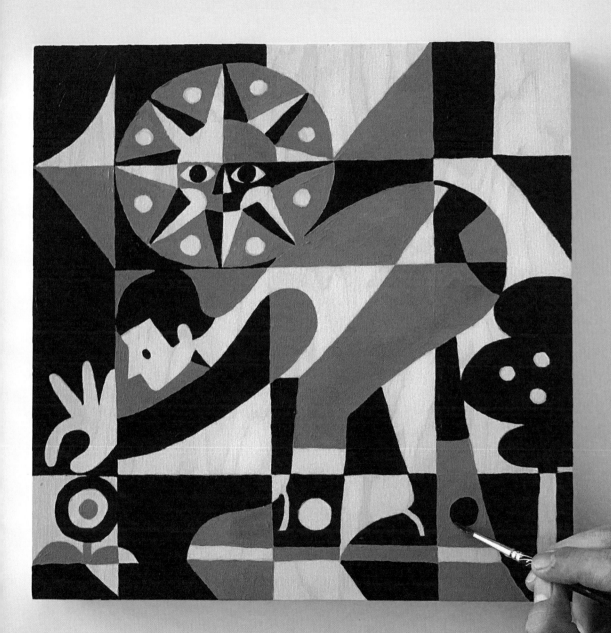

SUNDAY SUN NO. 145

PYEONGCHANG
2018 WINTER GAMES

2018
YEAR OF THE
DOG

Probably my favorite thing about people is their dogs.

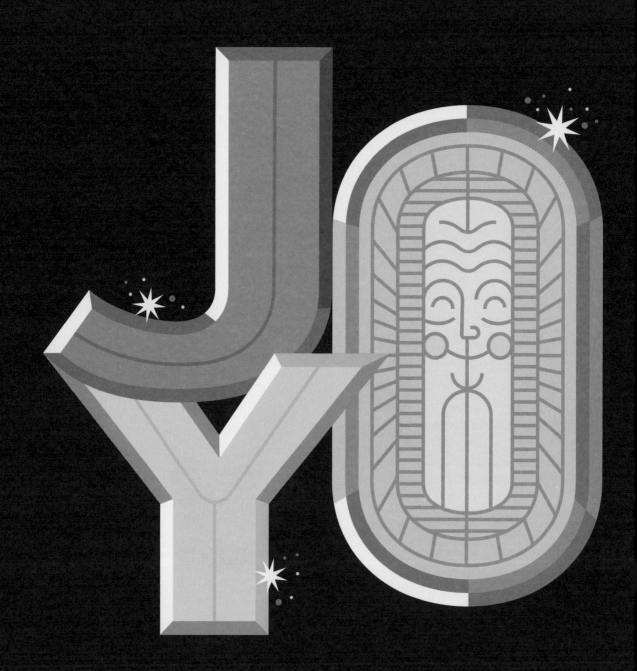

"I just love it when it snows."
Me, indoors drinking my
4th cup of organic free-trade
Ethiopian coffee.

In honor of all those ugly
sweaters. Happy Holidays.

WINTER

DREAM BIG

You call it procrastinating, I call it "creative research".

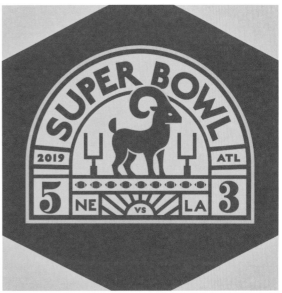

A four inch rib tattoo for
a friend. If you look close,
this design has the letters
"L" and "C" within it, for
my friend's spouse and son.

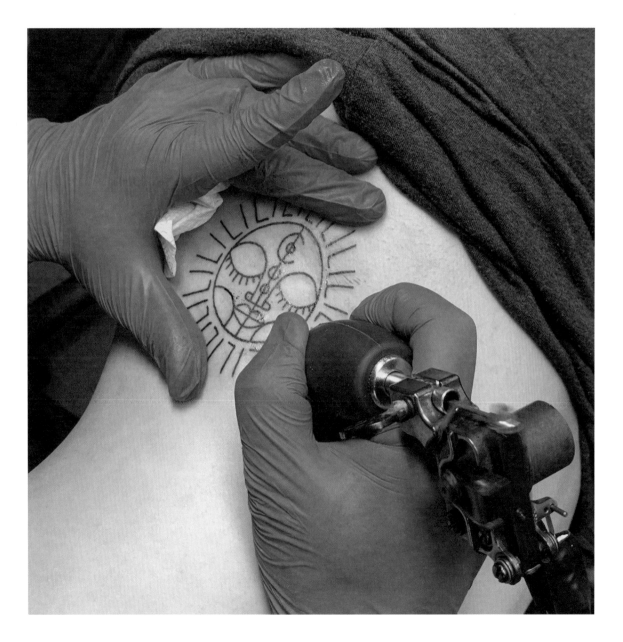

A limited edition three color RISO print.

Tad-SSNO. 197

Tad · SSNO. 196

In honor of a much-needed chill day.

Marriage is scrolling through Netflix looking for something to watch until you both just fall asleep.

The common advice to just go out and get a job that you love is misleading. No one was gonna pay me to sit in a comfy chair, eat pizza and watch Nicolas Cage movies. Graphic design is a wonderful alternative.

Interview
Tad Carpenter

How do you approach the blank page at the start of a new sun? Is this similar to beginning a client brief?

Very few of the suns I designed came with any real planning or strategy. I had several goals when I started this project, one was to practice my craft and the second was to do so in a set amount of time. I think doing this and not overthinking anything has helped alleviate any of that blank page fear. There is literally no time for it. Such a huge part of this project was trying to inspire and sharpen my skills. Similar to when a boxer trains for a fight, they do so with weighted gloves. Eventually, when that boxer enters the ring in a real fight the jabs they throw feel light, fast and easier to land. I had hoped, by restraining my time, that client work would also feel lighter, faster and easier to land. Part of the blank page fear, and this project, was simply learning to think fast, make decisions and persevere. Like all things, some days it comes easier than others. I've always thought design is a lot like a big roll of toilet paper. At first you're on a roll, then out of nowhere you're dealing with crap. You better be ready for it, learn to adapt and embrace that blank page, it's an invitation.

Could you describe the creative process you go through?

I actually create every one of these on Sunday. The majority of them are designed very, very early in the

morning before my family wakes up. It is an incredibly therapeutic process. Similar to my approach to client work, I start every sun with good old pencil and paper. I do my best thinking with my right hand. I draw fast, creating thumbnail sketches, exploring concept and composition. I try to spend more time on the idea than the execution of the design. That's not to say that some of my suns are not aesthetically driven. What can I say, I love a good symmetrical logo—sue me. I try to concept, design and share within two hours. I want these suns to be exploratory and spontaneous but inevitably many suns took on a life of their own and took much longer to complete. As the project grew, I found myself building sculptures, huge masks, routered wood signs, arranging photoshoots, screenprinting, painting, installing murals. I wanted to explore new ways to output my ideas and to do so with new materials, in new creative ways, became a huge part of the process.

How do you settle on a subject/theme?

When I start each sun, early on a Sunday morning, I do three things. Number one, I look in a tiny sketchbook I keep to see if I have any random ideas floating around in the margins—always save those golden gems that can get lost in the margins. Number two, I look at my calendar and at the news. Kind of simple but what is the date? Is it a holiday? A unique time of year? What is happening in the world or my life? Stopping and looking around yourself is more than enough to carry a concept and get you started quickly. Lastly, I ask myself how I feel. It could be in general or how I am feeling about one of those previously mentioned topics. To me, this project has been more therapy and introspection than anything. I truly hope people get a little joy, hope and kindness from my suns.

Your techniques are so varied. Is this a conscious decision or a reflection of how you would work in your design practice?

I would say a little bit of both. When working on each sun I deliberately wanted to experiment with new ways of communicating a concept. I strive for progress over perfection. Even when I work with clients I try very hard to push them outside of their comfort zones. That can be conceptually, how we position their brand or how we aesthetically design the work. I would always prefer trying something new and potentially failing, over duplicating something I have already done a hundred times.

"Design is like a big roll of toilet paper. At first you're on a roll and then out of nowhere you're just dealing with crap."

50% of being a dad is just breaking down cardboard Amazon boxes on trash night.

You're committed to creating a sun every week – what happens if you feel uninspired?

I am no different to anyone else. There are days when I feel like I left any motivation in my other pair of pants. But, this project has been a gift and something I look forward to every single week. I get to sit down and make something that did not exist on the planet the day before with no direction and no restrictions. It's incredibly easy to get motivated to sit down and play for an hour or two once a week.

Your designs are often created on the move, away from your home or the studio. How does your environment influence your work?

It really does. When I travel I do have to plan ahead a little for each sun. Sometimes it's as easy as just bringing a sketchbook with me on the road and finding time to draw for myself while traveling. Other times, I have done more experimental suns on the road. For example, drawing on an orange from my hotel room, painting on my hand or trying to plan ahead by making something before I travel. Like the one I made in Sydney, Australia. I painted that one at home and traveled with it until I found the right location to take the photo. In the end, having the Sydney Opera House in the background was perfect. As you can see, this project has become a personal journal for me. I can look at all of the suns and remember where I was when I made each one and how I was feeling.

Which sun gave you the most satisfaction?

This is always a hard question to answer. It is better than when I get asked, which sun is my favorite, which I also have a hard time answering. I will say, the most satisfying sun is Sun No. 173. Not because the design is all that special or even that the subject matter is overly poignant. This sun was made in collaboration with my mom. My mother is a fiber artist—more specifically a rug hooker. Rug hooking is an art made by dying your own wool and then pulling loops of that wool through a still linen or burlap base. She will never lose an opportunity to laughingly tell you, she is a hooker. I made this simple design and approached my mom to help me make it into a small hooked rug. She hand dyed the wool (she nailed the specific Pantone colors I wanted, of course) and hooked the piece for my sun. For that reason, this momma's boy will always hold this particular design very near and dear to his heart.

How are your personal values presented in your work?

When I created this project, I needed more positivity around me. Fast forward six years later, that feeling has only heightened. With that all said, my personal values and attributes are embedded in all of my work. Growing up the son of an illustrator, my dad opened up my world to whimsy, humor, cleverness, joy, inclusivity and fun. My father illustrated dozens of children's books, had a nationally syndicated comic-strip and was an art director and artist at Hallmark Greeting Cards for nearly 42 years.

> **"There are days when I feel like I left any motivation in my other pair of pants. But, this project has been a gift and something I look forward to every single week."**

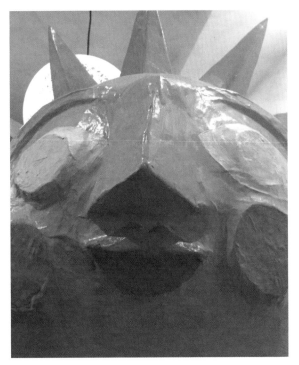

My dad's dedication to his craft, his work ethic and clever sense of humor are all values I've tried to model in my own work. In life, I think we all hope to somehow, someway make this place a little better. I hope in even the smallest, most minuscule way, my work can do that.

How does this personal project influence your commercial work?

This project has also created some amazing commercial opportunities and new projects that came to us because of my suns. A passion project should do two things for you. First it should allow you a space to explore. Creating a passion project creates structure to practice, to explore and grow. Defining a space to do that for me was crucial. The second thing it should offer is future opportunity. This wasn't the main reason I started SUNday Suns but quickly these suns were working as digital business cards. Potential clients were referencing them and contacting us because of them, which was very rewarding.

This project, was very much about self-exploration. However, when you do it for as long as I have done SUNday Suns, like all design it begins to offer opportunities to become collaborative. For me, I feel the best outcomes are normally those that are inclusive not exclusive. Many of my suns become opportunities to collaborate with people that I love. I worked with my wife Jessica countless times, my mom, dad, friends, strangers, you name it. Design at it's best brings people together. This project reminded me of that. During the week, as I work on commercial work and frankly just live my life, I try to think of opportunities where I can be a better collaborator with the people that I love and respect.

Design is easy. You just sit down at a computer, start drawing, clicking and poof 247 hours later you have one little OK thing.

Do you encourage your staff to do personal projects?

I do. I think all creatives should have something that is non-client driven that they are passionate about and want to pursue. Our culture has this "Rise and Grind" mentality that we always must be creating. Twenty-four-seven, earning and burning all day and night. Obviously, this is not healthy and your value as a human is not based purely on your output. Starting a personal project can be very helpful.

But then finish it, set a goal for yourself. Maybe a good personal project for us all is to learn to relax, and become curious about something outside of our profession. For me, hard work is addictive. That feeling of accomplishment and joy is intoxicating. With this project I set out to find a way to design a project that could help me with some of the issues I was facing. It did this. But in the end, my hope is that my suns better the experience for others and benefit them as much as it has benefited me.

What advice would you give to young creatives about maintaining personal projects?

I would recommend setting a strict structure to your project that you know you can achieve. For example, I knew I could not design a sun every single day, but once a week seemed much more attainable. Set structure and stick to it.

I would also recommend keeping the subject of your project as simple as possible to allow you room to be flexible. For me, the sun can mean so many things. It represents life, hope, joy, positivity, to some faith and life. But really, it was a simple symbol that allowed me to pour meaning back into it.

Besides the freedom this project has given you, what else have you learned from this experience?

I learned something new every week from this project. Subsequently, I also forgot five other things. This project has given me so much. It injected me

with a little hope each and every week, it really has made me look at things with a more positive lens. The project reminded me of how much I love to create and how important and therapeutic it can be. It also reminded me how important collaboration is when designing. Yes, this is a personal project, but so many of my favorite experiences were working with others.

My wife, Jessica as an example, she looked at every sun I designed every single SUNday critiquing them and helping me refine them and make them better. This project, like everything else in my life does not exist without her support, help and saint-like patience. They say marry someone better than yourself and I did that, times one hundred. I have worked with friends, parents and strangers over the six years of SUNday Suns. This project, like all projects, would be nothing without the collaboration and patience of others.

Do you see an artistic mission within your work?

I think I do, but it's hard to say when you are in such an active role in creating that work. I will say this, I've been in design long enough to know that you have no control over how things you make are received. I just want to get other opportunities to make good work.

That is my mission. I want to make work that is good and that betters the human experience. That's what design (or art) is at its core—a way for creatives to better this overall experience collectively. I really hope even one tiny thing I make can do that.

What are your ambitions for this project in the future?

The short answer, I have no idea. Design and passion projects are like little baby birds. You raise them, you feed them and then eventually you have to kick them out of the nest to fly on their own. You hope they grow up and sing lovely songs for people, opposed to just shitting on everything from 5,000 feet in the sky. I guess what I'm trying to say is I hope this project sings.

Counter-Print
© 2021 Counter-Print
counter-print.co.uk

British Library cataloguing-in-publication data:
A catalogue of this book can be found in the
British Library.

ISBN: 978-1-9161261-8-3

First published in the United Kingdom
in 2021 by Counter-Print.

Edited and produced by Counter-Print.

Copyright on projects and their related imagery
is held by Tad Carpenter.

All captioned quotes are by Tad Carpenter via his
Twitter account, @TadCarpenter.

Tad Carpenter
carpentercollective.com

Additional Credits:
Jessica Carpenter photographed: 51, 59, 60-61, 64-65,
66, 75, 85, 113, 116-117, 118, 122-123, 125, 132-133, 156-
157, 165, 166-167, 183, 187, 202, 207
Lauren Hakmiller photographed: 5, 57, 90
Bethany Hughes photographed: 2-3, 97, 209, 210-211
Becki Carpenter produced: 70, 72
Oxford Pennant produced: 17
Inch x Inch produced: 11
Throw + Co produced: 81
Vahalla Studios printed: 59, 84
Risotopia printed: 195

Design: Jon Dowling and Céline Leterme
Typefaces: Brown and Grouch
Printing and Binding: 1010 Printing
International Limited

This project could not be possible without
my partner and life-long creative collaborator,
Jessica Carpenter. Thank you for your time,
patience, skills and above all else your continued
love. I love you so.

—TC